CMStP&P #10253 Bi-Polar at Humpback Creek in the Cascades, 1924. James A. Turner.

Lawton Gowey Collection

A NORTHWEST RAIL PICTORIAL

with photographs
from the collection
of **Warren W. Wing**

Published by:
PACIFIC FAST MAIL
P.O. Box 57,
Edmonds, Washington
98020

Northern Pacific Q-5 class Pacific #2248 leaves Seattle's King Street station with a passenger train in the 1920's. Four other NP engines are in the background. The area at left is now occupied by the famous Kingdome.

© 1988   Second Printing
          Pacific Fast Mail

Library of Congress #83-61354

ISBN 0-915713-06-3 – hardbound edition
     0-915713-07-1 – softbound edition

Cover Photograph: James A. Turner

Book Design: Mike Pearsall

Lithographed in Hong Kong

Typography by:
The Type Merchant
Everett, Washington

The author and his son Dana with Norman and Dale Chester at the east end of the twin tunnels on the GN's old Cascade tunnel line. Photograph by Vernon Chester in 1962.

DEDICATION

This book is dedicated to my beloved Aunt Frank (Kate Frances Bach), an early and long-time resident of the South Seattle area. She was very influential in my becoming a railfan when she would give in to my pestering her for trips on interurbans and trains and more often for walks down to the railroad tracks. A summer was not complete without a week or two at her home. From her kitchen window I could watch all the trains and Puget Sound Electric Interurban traffic at the Southern end of Seattle. Those sights left an impression on me as a child that was to remain the rest of my life.

ACKNOWLEDGMENTS

"A NORTHWEST RAIL PICTORIAL" is a photo album of trains the author saw while growing up in Seattle. It is a collection of photographs taken by several well known Northwest rail photographers: Jim Fredrickson, Emery Roberts, Vernon Chester, Albert Farrow, and the late Lawton Gowey and Harold Hill. Also represented are photos taken by a little-known early-day rail photographer, the late James A. Turner, Seattle street car motorman and later trackless trolley driver. The earliest photos were taken by the late Edwin Little, an early-day telegrapher at the Great Northern station at Wellington.

Joining the above named are the works of more recent photographers William Bassler, Craig Williams, Kenneth Johnsen and Robert Johnston.

I am deeply grateful to these people for their cooperation in making this book possible. I have had hours and hours of dark room pleasure working with their negatives in the preparation. I am especially grateful to Mrs. Katherine Turner and her son James, who so generously loaned me negatives of Mr. Turner's collection over the years, and more recently in allowing me to purchase the collection.

As this is written, the author is saddened by the recent death of a very dear friend, Lawton Gowey. Lawton was, beyond a doubt one of the leading historians of Northwest electric railroads. He not only taught me the art of printing photos years ago but was also influential in my putting this book together.

Mention must also be made to those who loaned me timetables and maps, namely W. R. Grande, Don Dietrich, Victor Raffanelli and Jim Graves. Also, I want to express my appreciation to John Ritchie, past president of the Northwest Railfan Group, who went over each and every caption for accuracy.

Warren W. Wing
Seattle, Washington, 1983

Warren Wing

Six-year-old Mike Wing romps in the snow at Stampede Pass during a stop on the "Casey Jones" excursion to Cle Elum in 1962.

FOREWORD

This is a remarkable collection of photographs that chronicle not only the author's remembrances, but the entire history of rail transportation in the Puget Sound area. It spans a period of time from the arrival of the first transcontinental railroads to the dawn of the diesel age and Amtrak.

The collection is the result of one man's dedication to preserving that history, photographer and author Warren Wing, a Northwest native with a deep interest in trains and their impact on the region.

Born in Seattle in 1918, as a youngster Warren worked a newspaper route spending his spare change riding trains and trolleys. At the beginning of World War II, he enlisted in the U.S. Army, serving as a cook and later mess sergeant. He was assigned to troop movements and traveled from coast to coast, giving him further opportunity to ride and watch trains.

After the war, with his army service behind him, Warren joined the Postal Service as a letter carrier. It is interesting to note that he shared the same occupation with another rail photographer and collector, the legendary Otto Perry of Colorado narrow gauge fame. It was during his career with the Post Office that Warren began collecting photographs and meeting many of the photographers who are represented here.

What makes Warren Wing's collection so unique is its complete coverage of the railroads around Puget Sound in all eras, especially the 1920's, a period seemingly missed by many of the great rail photographers. Warren is indeed fortunate to have in his collection photographs from the brilliant Seattle photographer, James A. Turner. All rail enthusiasts and historians should be indebted to Turner for the trips he made into the "wilds" of the Cascades, to Stevens and Stampede Passes, to capture on film the trains of the 20's and 30's. To our knowledge this is the first time a large number of Mr. Turner's pictures have been published.

Of course there are other great Northwest rail photographers represented and the author graciously acknowledges them all. To each we would also like to extend our thanks and appreciation for sharing their work with us.

At one time the Northwest was served by four transcontinental railroads . . . the Great Northern, Northern Pacific, Union Pacific and the Milwaukee Road, plus smaller roads like the Pacific Coast Railway. The great stations, the "marble temples" of their age, Seattle's King Street, Union station and Tacoma's Union depot were never quiet. On their rails and beside their platforms stood the great trains of yesteryear . . . the Empire Builder, North Coast limited, Cascadian, Olympian to name only a few. Seattle's streets were criss-crossed by trolley and cable car lines and the big wood interurbans sped between Everett and Seattle; Seattle and Tacoma.

Most of this is gone now. And we sometimes wonder, as we sit in our automobiles trapped in an I-5 traffic jam, if their replacements are any better. We think not. That's why it is fun to look through Warren's collection. It brings us back to an earlier time when at every corner was a streetcar, and at every depot, a train.

In planning this book, we realized we could only use a small portion of Warren's magnificent collection. Hopefully there will be other books featuring his photographs. Knowing that more in-depth histories of the individual railroads have been done, we also attempted to keep this work simple, without lengthy text and just enough information in the captions to satisfy the most exacting rail buff. We felt that Warren's pictures have their own story to tell; not only for railfans but local residents as well who remember the great age of railroading in the Pacific Northwest.

The Editors
Pacific Fast Mail
Edmonds, Washington, 1983

James A. Turner

With his pack, canteen and camera gear, Photographer James A. Turner is ready for another trip into the Cascades. The scene is Corea, on the lower line of the Great Northern's Martin Creek loop, on June 28, 1925. The upper level can be seen directly above. Because of the danger of snowslides, the railroad's tracks between Scenic and Tye (formerly Wellington) were almost entirely covered by snowsheds.

TABLE OF CONTENTS

In the Mountains . . . . page   9
Along the Shore . . . . page   44
Salmon Bay Bridge . . . . page   57
Interbay . . . . page   62
In the Cities . . . . page   70
Argo Crossing . . . . page   90
Black River Junction . . . . page   98
Going South . . . . page 120
On the Peninsula . . . . page 140
The Interurbans . . . . page 146
Pacific Coast Railway . . . . page 152
Skagit Railway . . . . page 158

IN THE MOUNTAINS

NP Z-3 class Mallet #4005 helps push a freight over Stampede Pass on June 21, 1925. The car directly in front of the locomotive is one of the NP's ubiquitous round roof boxcars.

James A. Turner

9

This is one of the oldest photographs in the author's collection.
GN 2-6-0 #308 sits at what is believed to be Wellington,
Washington, on the west side of Stevens Pass, just after completion
of the railroad's extension to Puget Sound in 1893. The little Mogul
type locomotives were prime movers on the temporary switchbacks
until the opening of the original Cascade tunnel in 1900. The clue
to the photo's location is the covered enginehouse in the
background. One was known to have been located at Wellington in
the early days.

NP passenger train near the west portal of tunnel #4, 1920's.

Milwaukee Road passenger train eastbound in the Cascades.

Here are two rare early day Great Northern action photographs
taken by Clarence Gowey, father of the author's good friend, the
late Lawton Gowey. The location is near Index, Washington on
April 6, 1919 and depicts typical GN train operation in the
Cascades. Both the lead engine and mid-train helper are L-1 class
Mallets specially developed for service on the tough 2% grade
leading to Stevens Pass. The photographs are also interesting for
the old cars and the two little girls who seem oblivious to the
action. If you're wondering . . . the auto in the top photo approaching
the camera is a Chevy!

Edwin Little

A GN passenger train on the lower Martin Creek bridge approaching the famous Horseshoe tunnel. It was here the track made a complete semicircle to gain elevation; the upper level is directly above the train. This was one of the toughest stretches of track on the entire GN system and one of the reasons why the line was relocated and a new tunnel built at a lower elevation in 1929.

James A. Turner

Another was the constant maintenance needed on the many wood snowsheds, that protected the track from slides during the winter months. Here, in the 1920's, a GN work crew is busy building new sheds on the upper level of the Martin Creek loop.

James A. Turner

Further south, on Stampede Pass, the NP also employed a reverse loop to gain elevation. In these sequence photos, taken May 28th, 1926, the road's premier train, "The North Coast Limited" with a Pacific as road engine, and a Mikado as a helper, slowly makes its way around the loop on its approach to the west portal of Stampede tunnel.

James A. Turner

NP train #338 emerging from Stampede tunnel at Martin. The time
is 10:42 a.m. on September 5, 1925.

With two young railfans hitching a ride, two GN three-phase
electric's help a Mallet through the original Cascade tunnel. The
scene is at the east portal in 1925.

In the 1920's, as train length and tonnage increased, new and heavier locomotives were needed; especially in the rugged mountain passes of western Washington. The NP's answer was the Z-3 class 2-8-8-2 Mallet. Here, two of the mammoth engines help boost a long freight over Stampede Pass around 1924.

James A. Turner

James A. Turner

GN #2514 arrives at Tye with the Oriental Limited in 1924. An electric locomotive will couple on the head-end and take the train through the two-mile Cascade tunnel.

(above right) NP #4009 on Stampede Pass June 25, 1924.

A GN three-phase electric ready to be uncoupled at Cascade tunnel station after pulling a freight from Tye in the early 1920's.

James A. Turner

James A. Turner

James A. Turner

James A. Turner

James A. Turner

Tye, Washington (formerly Wellington) was a bustling community in 1924. It seems hard to believe all this would be gone a few years later. With the opening of the new Cascade tunnel in 1929, the old route through Tye and the original tunnel was abandoned.

(Upper left) NP Pacific #2108, with the Yakima local, makes its way up the west side of Stampede Pass in 1924.

GN 4-8-2 #2512 has just uncoupled from an electric locomotive at the west portal of the Cascade tunnel, August 10, 1924.

James A. Turner

NP #4025 at Lester, Washington July 24, 1937.

James A. Turner

A GN R class articulated works a long freight below Mt. Index in the 30's.

GN P-2 class 4-8-2 crossing Deception Creek in the 1930's.

James A. Turner

NP #4025 picking up orders at Stampede Station in the mid-20's.

James A. Turner

GN #1459 near Index, Washington with the "Cascadian" in tow.

James A. Turner

GN Electric #5003 and train at Dryden, Washington July 19, 1937.

James A. Turner

Craig Williams

Harold Hill

Craig Williams

James A. Turner

Here are several views taken around Scenic, Washington near the west portal of the Cascade tunnel. Left, GN electric #603 was used during construction of the new 11,000-volt line, and was later returned to the GN's interurban railroad, the Spokane, Coeur D'Alene and Palouse. Above left, GN Y-1 #5013 is eastbound with the "Cascadian," while a few years later (above) rebuilt #5011 is westbound with the same train. The addition of the highway #2 overpass in the top two photographs spoils the scene somewhat. The little depot at Scenic has long since been torn down.

James A. Turner

NP #1368 at Kanasket, Washington, westbound July 26, 1937.

Emery J. Roberts

NP Z-3 class #4008 at Cle Elum, Washington August 29, 1937.

Ed Gowey, Lawton Gowey Collection

CMStP&P special at Hyak, Washington. This is near the site of the
Milwaukee Ski Bowl. Many winter ski specials, powered by Bi-Polar
electrics, brought skiers to this popular spot in the 1940's.

GN Pacific #1459 has just uncoupled from the "Cascadian" at Skykomish. A class Y-1 electric locomotive will then take the train to Wenatchee. Both photos by Harold Hill.

GN Z class electrics 5006A and B on the "Cascadian" at Skykomish.

Harold Hill

Harold Hill

James A. Turner

James A. Turner

Another view of engine #1459 and train #6, the "Cascadian", with
Mt. Index forming a beautiful background.

(above left) GN #1453 heading eastbound from Monroe, Washington with the
"Cascadian" July, 1947.

(Left) GN O-5 class 2-8-2 #3300 heads a freight train through
Snohomish, Washington around 1930. The NP's Sumas line is
visible above the log car on the extreme right.

GN Mallet #2040 climbing
Stevens Pass on July 7, 1941, with
#3213 assisting. Both photographs
by James A. Turner.

Jim Fredrickson

NP train #4, the "Comet", westbound at Stampede tunnel station in 1945.

NP train #5 loading skiers at Martin in the winter of 1945.

CMStP&P Bi-Polar, leaving Pacific Coast Ry. trackage, eastbound on the "Bankers Ski Special" at Maple Valley, Washington February 22, 1947.

NP train #6, with three F units, climbs Stampede Pass in 1949. Compare this photograph with the earlier view of the Yakima local on page 20, taken at the same location.

CMStP&P Olympian Hiawatha in the Cascades. This photo was obtained from the Milwaukee Road when their offices were being closed in the Central Building in Seattle.

Warren Wing Collection

One of the Great Northern's huge class W electrics emerging from the "new" Cascade tunnel on April 12, 1956.

GN class W #5019 crosses an overpass in the Cascades, 1956.

William Bassler

Robert W. Johnston

Western Portal of the "new" Cascade tunnel in the 70's.

(left) The BN's "Empire Builder" eastbound at Skykomish in the early 1970's.

A quartet of Milwaukee Road Box cabs waits at Alberton,
Montana in the 1950's.

NP #2626, the Timken engine, on "Casey Jones" excursion at Cle Elum, Washington, August 4th, 1957.

ALONG
THE SHORE

GN #1457, near
Golden Gardens Park,
Seattle on September 6,
1948.

James A. Turner

GN #1459 crosses an overpass at Golden Gardens Park, Seattle.
Fort Lawton and the West Point lighthouse are just above the train.

James A. Turner

GN #1453 heading northbound along Puget Sound to Everett on
June 15, 1941.

James A. Turner

GN F-5 class 2-8-0 along Puget Sound.

James A. Turner

Swimmers greet the westbound "Cascadian" at Richmond Beach,
Washington in June, 1944.

Harold Hill

GN heavy Mikado #3215 on a
slightly overcast afternoon,
April 5, 1947.
James A. Turner

GN #2504 on the Empire Builder passes
Golden Gardens Park on July 2, 1936.
James A. Turner

GN #2050 southbound along
Puget Sound July 8, 1949.

James A. Turner

GN #1450 leaving Edmonds, Washington for Vancouver, B.C. with train #360 on June 24, 1950. The only landmark that hasn't changed in this scene is Standard Oil's pipeline bridge over the GN's tracks in the background.

NO PARKING HERE

Lawton Gowey

GN #1455 with the "International Limited" at Richmond Beach
June, 1944.

GN #511, an EMD class E-7, on the "International" near Seattle,
Washington. Photograph taken in 1949 by James A. Turner when
diesels were replacing steam on the train.

James A. Turner

GN's famous name train, the "Empire Builder," leaving Seattle on May 2, 1949.

GN #400 on an eastbound extra near Seattle on September 4, 1949.

James A. Tur...

(above right) A GN freight, northbound on May 4, 1945.

The "Empire Builder" enroute to Seattle.

James A. Turner

James A. Turner

SALMON BAY BRIDGE

After swinging down along the Sound, the GN's main line entered Seattle by crossing the Lake Washington ship canal on the massive Salmon Bay drawbridge. In 1938 engine #1452 approaches Ballard station with a passenger train. The hillside in the background is now covered by expensive homes and condominiums. The tug and log tow are about to enter Hiram Chittenden government locks.

James A. Turner

Train #360, with #1017
on the head end, crosses
Salmon Bay bridge on its
way to Vancouver
in the 20's.
James A. Turner

GN #2504 on train #1, the "Empire Builder," on the Salmon Bay bridge, about 7:30 in the morning, sometime in 1936.
James A. Turner

Magnolia Bluff and Ballard were still "way out in the country" when this view of the GN's "Oriental Limited" was taken around 1925. Ballard station was just across the bridge to the right. To say the area has changed somewhat would be putting it mildly!

James A. Turner

GN #1455 with the morning train to Vancouver, B.C. in the 1930's.

James A. Turner

GN #1724 passes Ballard station with a train for Spokane.

James A. Turner

In the 1920's the Great Northern operated train #278, a local from Seattle to Skykomish, that ran daily except Sunday. Power on the little train was usually B class American type #139. Photographer Turner, who lived in Ballard near the tracks, has captured the train emerging from the North Portal in Seattle, and several times on the Salmon Bay bridge. Note the huge GN "goat" herald on the counterweight.

INTERBAY

GN #505, an early F-1
class 2-8-0, heads a freight
through Interbay cut
on May 22, 1926.

James A. Turner

An early NP train passes Interbay and will soon cross over the ship canal to Fremont, the University District and on around the north end of Lake Washington to Woodinville. The GN's Salmon Bay drawbridge is at the extreme right background of the picture.

James A. Turner

GN #1244 at Ballard station in 1926. The locomotive still retained the old rectangular GN herald on the tender.

James A. Turner

Three well known classes of GN steam power pose at Interbay yards. Engine #1028 was an E-14 class ten-wheeler used in passenger service. Note the American flag on the cylinder cover. Engine #709 was one of the many 12-wheel type locomotives used by the GN. P-2 class Mountain type #2514 was used for many years on the GN's silk trains and name trains like the "Oriental Limited." All three photographs were taken by James A. Turner in the 1920's.

GN O-4 Mikado #3213 at Interbay, with a Fort Lawton streetcar right above the locomotive. Taken in the late 20's by James A. Turner.

GN 0-8-0 switcher #871 works Interbay yards in 1939.

Harold Hill

A big R-2 class Mallet heads east from Interbay in the 1930's.

James A. Turner

GN #1371 on NP Interbay trestle after crossing Lake Washington ship canal. The GN's Salmon Bay bridge was closed for repairs at this time, June 14, 1948.

Lawton Gowey

GN #1363 backing to Interbay after bringing a train to King Street Station.

Harold Hill

James A. Turner

GN #2054, near Interbay,
April 21, 1949.

James A. Turner

The GN's "Empire Builder"
in Interbay cut,
Seattle in 1950.

IN THE CITIES
SEATTLE/TACOMA

4th Avenue South in Seattle, looking north from Jackson Street around 1930. The #19 route carline was the last line to operate, converting to buses in April, 1941.

James A. Turner

Seattle Municipal Street Railway at Pioneer Square, 1st and Yesler Way in 1923. The buildings and famous landmarks are still there. .

GN A-9 class switcher #381 was the King Street passenger car shifter in 1926.

James A. Turner

The Great Northern's "Empire Builder" arriving at King Street.

Seattle Electric's car #372 on the Fremont to Ballard shuttle, at 20th NW and Ballard Avenue around 1910.

James A. Turne

A Seattle & Rainier Valley car at 4th and Pine in downtown Seattle in the early 30's. The GN sign above Sullivan's Florist shop was there for many years.

James A. Turner

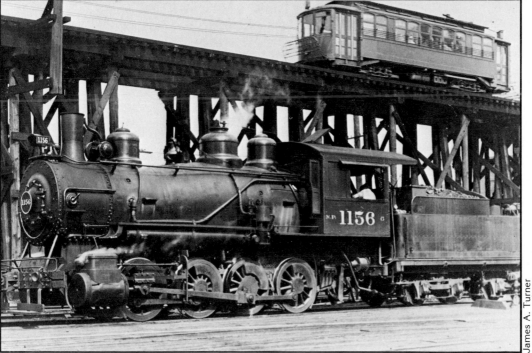

James A. Turner

(above) NP #1505 was used as a helper on Stampede Pass and later on the Auburn to Seattle transfer in the mid-20's.

(lower) NP Switcher #1156 on Seattle's waterfront in 1925. The streetcar on the elevated line is outbound for West Seattle or Lake Burien.

CMStP&P 0-6-0 #1245 behind Sears Roebuck in Seattle, July 3, 1924.

CMStP&P #7057 just south of Spokane Street, Seattle in the mid-30's.

Lawton Gowey Collection

3rd Avenue in Seattle, looking north from Yesler Way in October, 1926. The King County Courthouse is on the right.

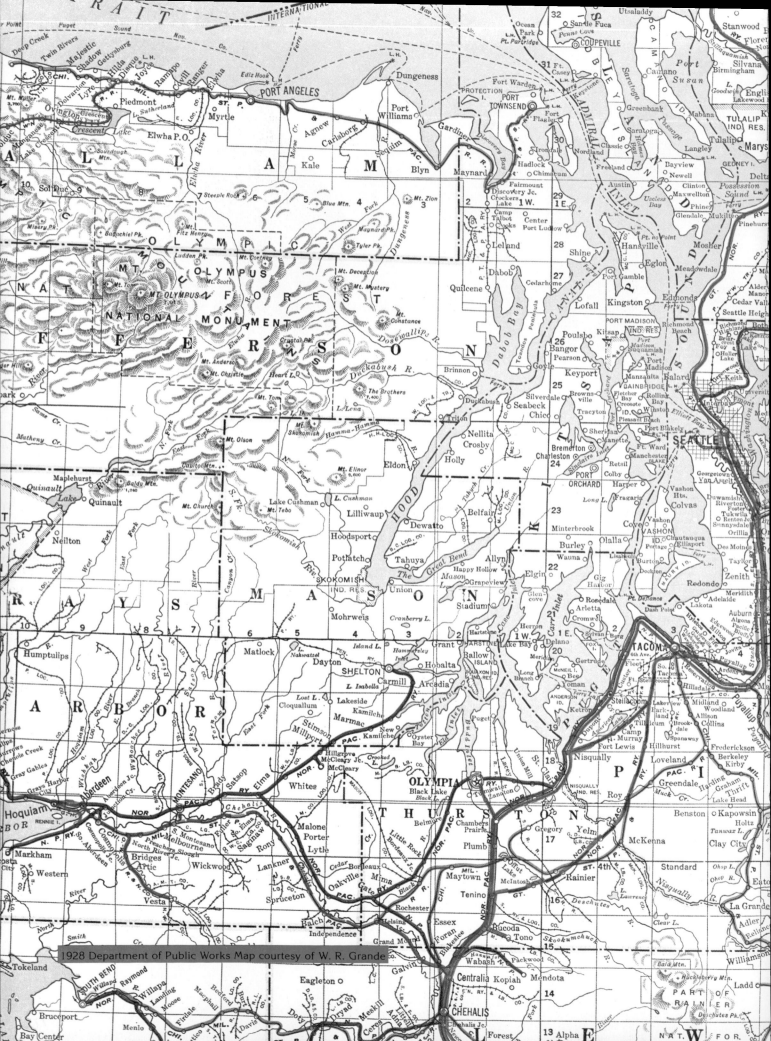

1928 Department of Public Works Map courtesy of W. R. Grande

GN #1008 arrives at King Street Station. Seattle & Rainier Valley streetcar is inbound on 4th Avenue South on the way down to its terminal at Stewart Street.

James A. Turner

UP 4-6-2 #3201 on the front of #561, the Portland train, waits at Seattle. Over the boiler of the locomotive can be seen the pole and roof of a 300 series type streetcar of the Seattle & Rainier Valley Railway. Taken in 1925 by James A. Turner.

NP #2194 pushing the #2216 into
the Stacy Street roundhouse.

James A. Turner

NP #2247 crossing Spokane Street, Seattle. The Smith Tower is
barely visible in the background. It was unusual to see a double
header on so short a train, but it may be going to pick up
additional cars at East Auburn.

James A. Turner

SMStRy car #9 on the Yesler Way cable at the 3rd Avenue
terminal in 1939.

James A. Turner

Another view of busy Spokane Street, this time with a big NP class A
4-8-4 on the head end. The Puget Sound Electric trestle can be
seen to the right of the locomotive. NP and GN trains sailed across
Spokane Street nonstop whereas UP and Milwaukee Road trains, because
of having to cross the NP's wye tracks, had to stop both ways.

James A. Turner

Car #319 of the Seattle Municipal Street Railway on the Queen Anne counterbalance. A heavy counterbalance ran underground going the opposite way of the car. Attendants were stationed at the top and bottom of the grade to attach the car to the weight. At night only one attendant was on duty and he would ride the cars up and down the hill. During the days of two-man operation the conductor did the attaching. Oldtime residents have told the author that the hill was the place to test new autos. If they went up the hill, you knew you didn't get a lemon!

The Seattle Municipal Street Railway served Seattle and its suburbs for many years. In a stunning photograph by James A. Turner, car #573 sits at the outer end of the Sunset Hill line at W. 64th and 36th NW, with the Sound and Olympic Mountains forming a perfect backdrop. The man in overalls was a familiar sight on the cars over the years; he was the systems track greaser. March 29, 1939

SMStRy car #807 on the Fort Lawton line. The car is on Government Way on its way downtown from the army's Fort Lawton. It's January and there's a bit of snow on the ground but not enough to hinder street operations. The big snow of February, 1916 is best remembered by oldtimers when everything was tied up for days.

Lawton Gowey Collection

James A. Turne

SMStRy double-truck Birney car #756 passing through
Woodland Park in Seattle in the 1930's. The line was
operated counterclockwise around Green Lake. It was
lightly patronized, but popular with sightseers.

(above right) NP #2264 with the Spokane morning train on July 13, 1941.

The UP's first streamliner, the M-10,000, on exhibit in Seattle's
Union Station, 1934.

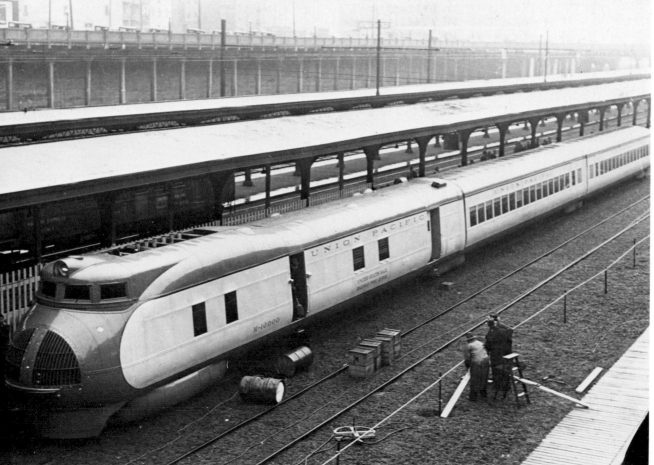

Craig Williams

James A. Turner

Seattle & Rainier Valley car #101 riding along Lake Washington on its way from Seattle to Renton in the early 30's. Service ended in 1936 and the right-of-way is now occupied by expensive homes. The car was built by Moran shipyards in Seattle and had looks only a diehard trolley fan could love!

Milwaukee Road's "Olympian" loading at Union Station in Seattle.

Warren Wing Collection

Argo Crossing was a busy place in the 1920's, and was the author's favorite spot to watch trains. This photo was taken on January 18, 1914 and shows Seattle Electric's car #327 crossing Argo, southbound to Georgetown. It will soon join the Puget Sound Electric and go about 4 or 5 blocks to where the interurban and streetcar lines part, the trolley going across the Duwamish River to South Park, and the interurban south to Renton and Tacoma. At the far left is the UP's roundhouse and freight yards. Next is the Puget Sound Electric's double track to 1st Avenue in downtown Seattle. The five tracks are from left to right, the CMStP&P, Pacific Coast, NP freight trackage, and the NP's main line from King Street. The tracks between the small building and the feed mill are the Milwaukee-UP tracks from Union Station.

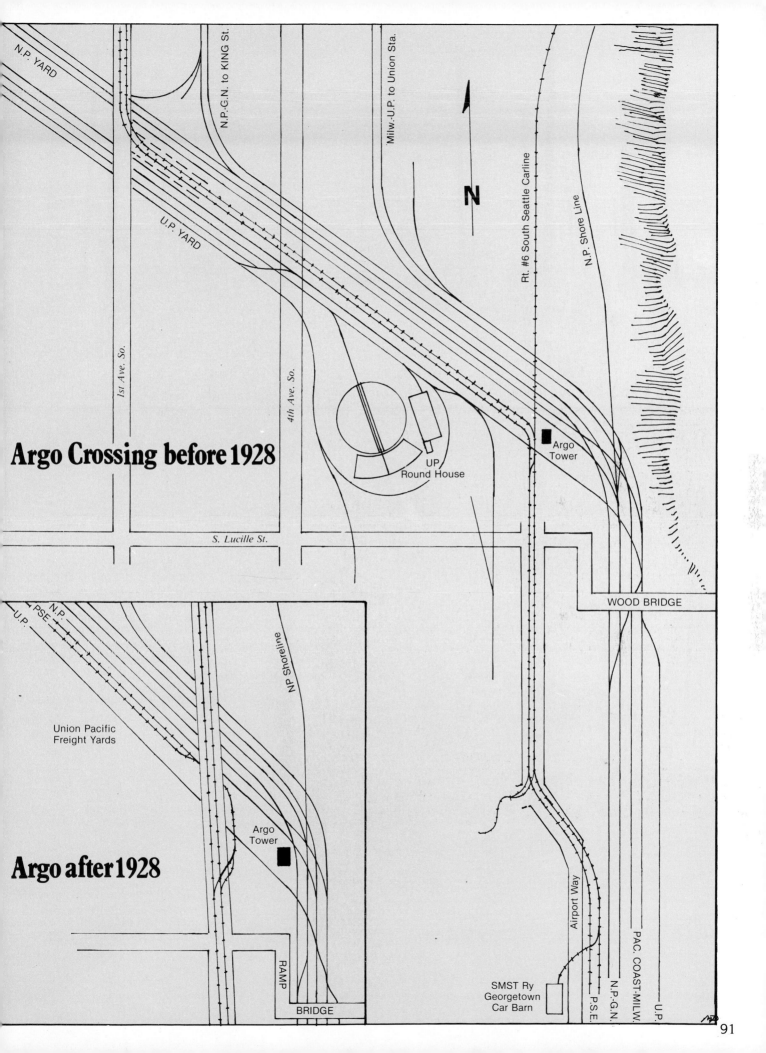

Argo Crossing before 1928

N.P. YARD

N.P.-G.N. to KING St.

U.P. YARD

Milw.-U.P. to Union Sta.

Rt. #6 South Seattle Carline

N.P. Shore Line

N

1st Ave. So.

4th Ave. So.

UP Round House

Argo Tower

S. Lucille St.

WOOD BRIDGE

PAC. COAST-MILW.

Argo after 1928

N.P.

PSE

U.P.

Union Pacific Freight Yards

NP Shoreline

Argo Tower

RAMP

BRIDGE

Airport Way

SMST Ry Georgetown Car Barn

P.S.E.

N.P.-G.N.

PAC. COAST-MILW.

U.P.

Warren Wing Collection

James A. Turner

(above)
An ex-Minneapolis car on the Sea[
Municipal Railway is about to cros[
the Milwaukee tracks. Notice the [
conductor about to flag the street[
across the busy tracks of the stea[
roads. The Globe Feed Mills burne[
in 1928 causing a huge loss in gr[
and the lives of 14 horses. The
author was at the scene and
remembered that streetcar and au[
traffic was halted for quite some t[

The UP's train to Portland, with
engine #3225 must be causing a
traffic jam as it waits for clearance
at Argo on April 14, 1925.

NP #2184 on the northside of Argo Crossing, Seattle in the 1920's.

CM&StP #6000 arrives at Argo and waits for clearance to proceed to Union Station, 1924.

Craig Williams

NP Switcher #1097 south across UP tracks at Argo.

The NP's morning train to Grays Harbor waits at Argo in 1924.

James A. Turner

Argo Crossing was 3.2 miles south of Seattle's King Street station.
Here is NP train #2 at Argo on June 28, 1924. It left Seattle at 9:15 a.m.

Warren Wing Collection

James A. Turner

Chicago Milwaukee & St. Paul #2709 on train #1, the "National
Park Limited" waiting for clearance at Argo Crossing on July 22,
1924. The train had left Union Station at 7:30 a.m. and arrived at
Argo 10 minutes later. It was scheduled to arrive at Ashford at
10:45. It returned to Seattle at 7:15 p.m.

Argo Crossing in 1971 with a UP freight about to cross the BN tracks. Puget Sound Electric's interurbans formerly crossed the UP behind the locomotive and tower and turned left into double track at the location of the Argo sign.

Robert W. Johnston

Robert W. Johnston

Amtrak's "Coast Starlight" approaching Argo in the 70's.
Milwaukee-UP tracks on the extreme right; NP, Milwaukee, PC,
freight tracks to the left of the train. The Puget Sound Electric
double track was just left of center; UP freight yards on the left.

Robert W. Johnston

The Empire Builder of the 1970's at Argo Crossing en route to Chicago.

James A. Turner.

BLACK RIVER JUNCTION

located just south of Boeing Field in Seattle, and where all the major railroads serving the city converged, was a busy place during the steam era. Here NP #2241 on the Spokane morning train is southbound by Black River in the 1930's. Track on extreme right goes east to Renton and on up the east shore of Lake Washington to Woodinville and Sumas.

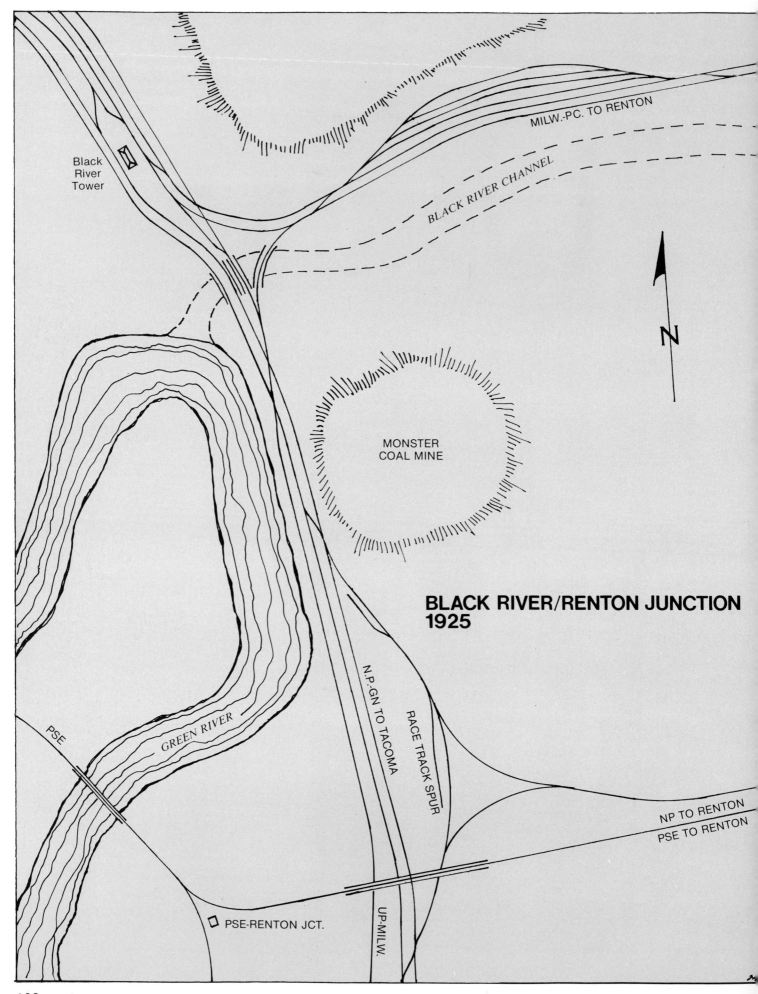

Black
River
Tower

MILW.-PC. TO RENTON

BLACK RIVER CHANNEL

N

MONSTER
COAL MINE

**BLACK RIVER/RENTON JUNCTION
1925**

N.P.-GN TO TACOMA

RACE TRACK SPUR

PSE

GREEN RIVER

NP TO RENTON

PSE TO RENTON

PSE-RENTON JCT.

UP-MILW.

UP #2510 at Black River on June 3, 1944. NP main line is on the right.

James A. Turner

James A. Turner

UP #7014 under Milwaukee Road catenary at Black River,
September 6, 1950. Milwaukee main line going east on the right.

An NP train branches off the main at Black River for Renton and up the Lake line. Note conductor with the order hoop on his arm.

James A. Turner

Pacific Coast Railway #12 passes the switching tower at Black River Junction, in the 1930's.

James A. Turner

NP #227 with the Grays Harbor morning train, April 10, 1939.

James A. Turner

CMStP&P #10253 passing through Black River yards west of Renton en route to Seattle in the mid-20's.

James A. Turner

NP #1384, an S-4 class ten-wheeler at Black River, Washington on August 17, 1951. Train is on the Lake line; the main line is seen just above the locomotive. The trackage from Black River through Renton is now abandoned. The Lake line now connects with the old Pacific Coast Newcastle line in North Renton.

Albert Farrow

Warren Wing collection.

Great Northern morning train for Portland, leaving Seattle, July 1967.

CMStP&P "Olympian" with Fairbanks-Morse #9 loading at Tacoma
Station, August 15, 1947.

William Bassler

Robert C. Myers from the K.G. Johnsen Collection

The "reserved seat" coach of the
Tacoma-East Auburn connecting train is nudged by little
NP 0-6-0 #1083 at Tacoma's Union Station in 1953.

NP #2602 on the noon train from Seattle, leaving Tacoma's Union
Station. The photograph by Emery Roberts was taken on
June 1, 1946, from the 15th Street bridge.

A classic railroad photograph. NP Q-6 class 4-6-2 #2262 departs
Tacoma's Union Station with train #415 on May 18, 1954, for
connection at East Auburn.

Albert Farrow

Jim Fredrickson

NP #2626, the Timkin engine, brings the mid-day Seattle to
Portland train into Tacoma depot on April 9, 1952.

Albert Farrow

CMStP&P Bi-Polar on train #16 loading at Tacoma, April 15, 1949.

Here is a couple of pictures taken by Jim Fredrickson on a cold and snowy day in Tacoma. NP #1782 is on a caboose hop. It will pick up a coach and return to East Auburn to meet train #5. Meanwhile, NP train #415, with engine #1381 is leaving for East Auburn in 1952.

(right) NP #1906 at Reservation (Tacoma), Washington with a logging transfer, April 23, 1954. Union Pacific trackage in center with Milwaukee main line across Puyallup River.

NP #1548 at Tacoma
in the summer of 1953.
Schoenfeld's Furniture store
with its two-story high letters
is still there, but the
locomotive and heavyweight
cars are long gone.

Robert C. Myers from the KG. Johnsen Collection

Albert Farrow

CMStP&P #53 backing train into Tacoma yards, March 4, 1948.
This 2-6-6-2 Mallet was used on the former Tacoma Eastern.

GN #3131 heads through South Tacoma with a local freight in the 30's.

Emery J. Roberts

William Bassler

Albert Farrow

114

Albert Farrow

NP #1365 at Reservation (Tacoma), Washington coming in on the
Enumclaw local, May 17, 1956. The Puget Sound Electric crossed
Puyallup and NP main line just to the right of the highway bridge.

(above left) CMStP&P E-23 class electric at Tacoma's new station, July 29, 1956.

(left) CMStP&P E-1 arrives at old Tacoma depot on Puyallup and Pacific
Avenues in the early 1950's. Notice the inspection cars in the foreground.

William Bassler

UP morning train from Portland at Tacoma in the mid-1950's.

(above right) CMStP&P E-23 electric on the "Olympian" at Seattle's Union Station. This engine was converted from a box motor replacing the famous Bi-Polar.

(right) With the Burlington Northern merger, interesting and different motive power with a variety of color schemes began appearing in the Puget Sound area. Here, an EMD E-8 of Burlington ancestry brings in the morning train from Portland on November 15, 1971.

Jim Fredrickson

Albert Farrow

A special excursion from Portland arriving at Tacoma via the Prairie Line. It returned to Portland by way of Olympia and Gate, June 27, 1971.

(lower left) CMStP&P E40 at Tacoma yards, July 31, 1953.

Amtrak's "Coast Starlight" boarding at King Street station. Compare this scene with some of the earlier views.

Robert W. Johnston

GOING SOUTH

CMStP&P #1225 on the Sumner, Washington covered bridge, March 3, 1943.

Albert Farrow

James A. Turner

UP #7818 on a southbound Portland train in the 30's.

Harold Hill

NP #1713 northbound at Milwaukee Road and Pacific Coast crossover in Renton, 1951.
This line was abandoned at the time of the BN merger and is now a parking lot.

CMStP&P 10250 with a Tacoma-bound train under the Allentown
covered bridge.

James A. Turner

NP train #5 with #2260 leaving Ellensburg westbound. August 18, 1940.

Emery J. Roberts

Warren Wing collection.

The Milwaukee Road's "Olympian Hiawatha" cuts through a typical
Northwest mist for a station stop at Renton, Washington in 1961.

James A. Turner

UP morning passenger train from Portland. Milwaukee Road catenary on the right.

James A. Turner

NP #2608, inbound from Spokane, under the Allentown covered bridge in the 1930's.

James A. Turner

NP Gas-electric B-19 on the Grays Harbor train heading by Boeing Field, Seattle.

(above right) CMStP&P 10500 on Railroad Avenue in Renton, Washington in the 1930's. The double track through Renton was later reduced to one.

(right) CMStP&P 10254 by Allentown underpass, 9 miles south of Seattle.

James A. Turner

NP #2263 southbound by Georgetown carbarn, April, 1938.

UP #7017 was used on many of the UP's important trains. Here it is at Centralia, Washington on the Seattle-Portland pool train on September 9, 1952.

William Bassler

Albert Farrow

NP switcher #1098 on the Olympia log dump track on July 19, 1955. Washington State capitol in the background with NP line to Grays Harbor just below.

CMStP&P Box Cab #10510 prepares to head south from Van Asselt yard, near Boeing Field, Seattle, in 1934. The photograph was taken by James Turner from the parallel right-of-way of the Union Pacific.

NP #2260 on train #4 at East Auburn with #2185 and the Tacoma connection on the adjoining track, 1946.

Jim Fredrickson

Freshly shopped Milwaukee Road 2-8-0 #7239 drifts through
Allentown, en route to Seattle, with a logging transfer on
August 26, 1937.

Albert Farrow

CMStP&P E-22 on freight to Seattle in 1951. Taken from Allentown covered bridge. I-5 now crosses at this location.

(above right) NP #1823 on a Ringling Brothers/Barnum & Bailey circus train at Auburn, Washington August 22, 1948.

NP #2262 leaving Centralia, Washington for Seattle, April 30, 1939. UP #2169 on the siding at left and photographer Harold Hill taking his shot on the right.

Rebuilt Milwaukee Road Box Cab with a Geep helper on a long freight, south of Seattle.

Warren Wing collection.

Amtrak's "Empire Builder" at Yakima, June 1975.

NP #1776 on last steam train through Nisqually, Washington December 8, 1957. This was on a "Casey Jones" excursion to Centralia. The line went on to Aberdeen and Hoquiam and up the Washington coast to Moclips. This particular branch, Hoquiam to Moclips, had not seen passenger service for many decades.

Warren Wing

NP #2261 on train #461 at Olympia, Washington February 14, 1956. The last trip was made four days later. Train was en route from Seattle to Hoquiam.

Jim Frederickson

NP mixed train for Raymond and South Bend, Washington standing
at Centralia depot in the early 1950's.

William Bassler

NP #2626, the famous "Timken" engine on train #422 to Tacoma.
The 2626 was a replacement for the regular engine which had broken down.

Jim Fredrickson

James A. Turner

NP diesel #6504 on a train bound for Spokane, June 30, 1949.

Kenneth G. Johnsen

NP FT's roll a freight along Burnett Street in Renton in the late 1960's.

Train #406 on Tacoma drawbridge detour, January 22, 1967.
The Point Defiance line was closed by a slide and the train rerouted
to Portland via Prairie Line.

Jim Fredrickson

GN geep #603 on special excursion on Maple Valley trestle
en route to Black Diamond, September 13, 1958.

Lawton Gowey

ON THE PENINSULA
NP #1621
and train #591 at
Raymond,
Washington.

Jim Fredrickson

Harold Hill

Harold Hill

NP W3 class 2-8-2 #1752 by the freight depot at Shelton, Washington in 1950.

NP Gas-electric B-8 waits at Gate, Washington for 4-6-2 #2194 with the Grays Harbor train. The B-8 is the Centralia connection, and will leave right after the 2194 pulls out for Olympia and Seattle.

NP train #596 with engine #1621 on last trip to South Bend,
Washington in March, 1954.

Another view of NP #1776 on the last steam operation from Seattle
with the "Casey Jones" excursion, December 8, 1957.

NP B-18 gas electric unloading express at South Bend, Washington
on August 11, 1929.

THE INTERURBANS

A classic photograph from
the great days of the heavy wood
interurbans. Puget Sound Electric's
#512 and #529 are facing South
on 1st Avenue by the Sears mail
order plant, around 1915. Car #529
was originally an open-end
observation extra-fare trailer
later motorized. Both cars ran
until the end of service in 1928.
PSE cars were dual equipped with
trolley poles for city operation
and third rail shoes for the country.
Local trains left Seattle on the hour,
with Limiteds on the half hour.

PSE cars #502, #507 and an unidentified trailer pose along the right-of-way. The motorized cars were worn out by steady use and high speeds by 1910. The trailers were in service right until the end. A few saw additional service on Seattle's City Light Skagit River Railway.

PSE #559 standing at Renton Junction in 1915. The crew is motorman Howard Wellman and conductor Horace Rumery. Wellman was the first motorman hired and with conductor Rumery ran the last car to Renton on Saturday night, December 29, 1928. Barn at left advertised your credit was good at Standard Furniture Company at 2nd and Pine in Seattle. The sign is gone but the barn was still standing in late 1982.

Harold Hill

North Coast Lines, ex-Pacific Northwest Traction's car #55 is northbound through Alderwood Manor in 1938. This was one of the last cars to run in February, 1939. The Right-of-way is still very much in evidence, some of it right alongside I-5.

Car #55 crossing Highway #99 on its way to Everett in 1939.

Another view of car #55, southbound at 105th and Evanston in
1938, with motorman Johnson at the controls. The house at left
was owned by the descendants of early Seattle banker, Dexter
Horton. They were friends of the author's grandmother, and in the
20's she would ride out in her 1916 Ford for a visit, accompanied
by the author and his brother. While grandmother was visiting, the
brothers would sit on the log and watch the big interurbans roll by.

Albert Farrow

Traction returns to Seattle! Under the guidance of Councilman
George Benson, Seattle's new waterfront trolley, with three former
Melbourne, Australia cars, opened on Memorial Day in 1982. The
operation has been so successful that there's talk of extending the
line and even opening new routes. That's Amtrak's
Empire Builder arriving in Seattle at the right.

Albert Farrow

THE PACIFIC COAST RAILWAY

The Pacific Coast Railway was formerly the Seattle & Walla Walla Railroad, a three-foot gauge line, incorporated in 1873 to connect the cities in its title by way of Renton and Snoqualmie Pass. In 1880 Henry Villard of Northern Pacific fame, formed the Columbia & Puget Sound to purchase and complete the S&WW. In 1897 Villard's railroad properties were purchased by the Pacific Coast Co. and converted to standard gauge. The 33-mile line which ran from Seattle through Renton, Maple Valley and Black Diamond to Franklin, became the Pacific Coast RR in 1916. In 1951 the road was sold to the Great Northern.

PC #16, a 2-8-0, passes under the Allentown covered bridge on September 14, 1951. The picturesque bridge was burned by arsonists in 1961. I-5 now crosses at this location.

Warren Wing Collection

A rare early view of Columbia & Puget Sound #18 at New Castle about 1910. In the background is one of the coal mines that was originally owned by Henry Villard when he formed the C&PS.

James A. Turner

PC passenger engine #18 loading at Seattle Station, Railroad Avenue & King Street, in 1924. No. 18 was later used in freight service, then stored in a waterfront roundhouse until it was scrapped in 1939, with the scrap going to Japan. In the background is the elevated streetcar trestle to West Seattle.

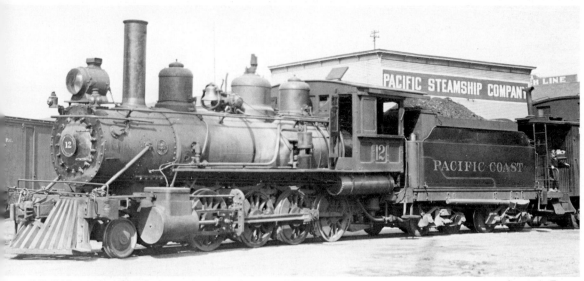

PC #12 on the Seattle waterfront in the mid 20's.

James A. Turner

PC 0-6-0 #17 switches the Seattle yards on July 1, 1948.

James A. Turner

PC #15 at Taylor in 1943 with engineer Miller leaning on the front coupler. Miller lived on the author's mail route in Seattle and was always good for a railroad yarn when out by his mail box. Miller told the author that from time to time he'd let young firemen run the engine, but cautioned them about handling the cars too rough, as they might bang themselves out of a job!

Harold Hill

PC #16 switching at Maple Valley in 1939. The branch to Taylor is on the left with the Milwaukee Road's main line between the locomotive and coal cars. Maple Valley was a busy railroad junction until the Taylor branch was abandoned in 1944 and coal shipments declined from Black Diamond. Passenger service was provided for many years to Black Diamond and Taylor.

PC #14 and 15 detour through Auburn over the NP because of a washout on PC trackage.

Albert Farrow

PC #15 in the hole at Renton in the 1940's waiting for the
Milwaukee's E-25 to clear. Milwaukee leased the PC's trackage from
Maple Valley to Argo.

Harold Hill

SRRy motor #1626 at Newhalem on August 30, 1953, trails cars from the Puget Sound Electric and the Oregon Electric.
Warren Wing Collection

Skagit River Ry. little 2-6-2 #6 waits at City Light's Newhalem camp. The line ran from Rockport along the Skagit River to Newhalem, and on up to Diablo.
Warren Wing Collection

SRRy in the 1920's. Seattle City Light had a special excursion from Newhalem to Diablo.

Warren Wing Collection

SKAGIT RAILWAY

Seattle City Light's Skagit Railway connected with the Great Northern's branch at Rockport, Washington. In the background engine #6 does some switching. The trailer car is thought to be off the old Puget Sound Electric.
Warren Wing Collection

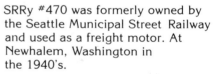

SRRy #470 was formerly owned by the Seattle Municipal Street Railway and used as a freight motor. At Newhalem, Washington in the 1940's.

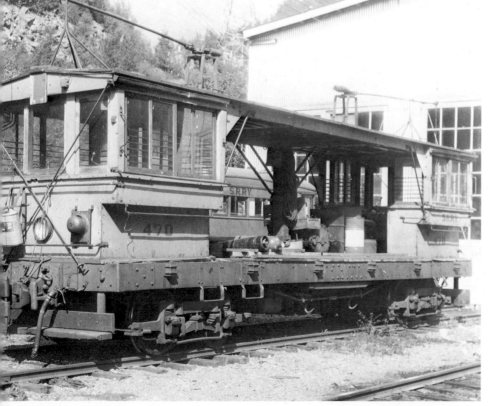

Warren Wing Collection

INDEX

AMTRAK *40, 96-97*

BURLINGTON NORTHERN *41, 135*

GREAT NORTHERN
Locomotives, steam
0-6-0   #381 *72*
0-8-0   #871 *66*
2-6-0   #308 *11*
2-8-0   #505 *62-63*, #1105 *47*, #1244 *64*
2-8-2   #3300 *32*, #3215 *48*, #3213 *34, 66*,
        #3131 *113*
2-6-6-2 *12*
2-6-8-0 *16*
2-8-8-2 *22*, #2043 *35*, #2050 *48-49*,
        #2054 *67, 69*
4-4-0   #139 *61*
4-6-0   *13*, #1017 *58*, #1008 *80*, #1028 *65*
4-6-2   #1459 *25, 30-31, 33, 46*,
        #1453 *32, 46*,
        #1457 *45, 47*, #1450 *50-51*,
        #1455 *52, 60*, #1452 *56-57*,
        #1724 *60*, #1371 *68*, #1363 *68*
4-8-0   #709 *65*
4-8-2   #2514 *18, 65*, #2512 *20*, #2516 *24*
        #2504 *49, 59*, Oriental Ltd. *58-59*,
        (unnumbered) *21*, #2503 *73*

Locomotives, electric
Three phase   *16, 19*
Y-1   #5003 *25*, #5013 *26*, #5011 *27*
Class Z   #5006A&B *31*
Class W   *39, 40*

Locomotives, diesel
F-units   *53*, #400 *54*, #251 *55*
E-units   #511 *52*
Geep   #603 *139*
SDP40 *105*

MILWAUKEE ROAD
Locomotives, steam
0-6-0   #1245 *80*
2-8-0   #7057 *80*, #1225 *120-121*, #7239 *131*
2-6-6-2   #53 *112*
4-6-2   #6000 *93*, #2709 *95*

Locomotives, electric
Bi-polar   #10253 frontpiece *103*, #10250 *123*,
       (numbers unknown) *29, 27, 108, 114, 117*,
       #10254 *127*
Box-cabs   *42*, #E-14 *114, 118, 127, 134, 157*,
       #E-22 *132*, #10510 *130*

Locomotives, diesel
FM   #9 *106*

NORTHERN PACIFIC
Locomotives, steam
0-6-0   #1097 *94*, #1098 *129*, #1083 *106*
0-8-0   #1156 *75*
2-8-2   #1599 *15*, #1505 *75*, #1782 *110*,
        #1540 *111*, #1906 *111*, #1713 *122*,
        #1682 *137*, #1621 *141*, #1752 *142*,
        #1621 *144*, #1776 *136, 145*, #1823 *133*
2-8-8-2   #4005 *8-9*, #4011 & #4008 *17*,
        #4008 *28*, #4009 *19* #4025 *23, 24*
4-6-0   #1368 *28*, #246 *94*, #227 *103*,
        #1381 *110*, #1365 *115*, #1384 *104*
4-6-2   #2248 *2-3*, #2310 *16*, #2108 *20*,
        #2194 *142* W/2216 *81*, #2247 *81*,
        #2264 *87*, #2184 *93*, #2107 *95*,
        #2241 *98-99*, #2262 *108*,
        #2263 *128, 133*, #2260 *123, 130*,
        #2261 *136*
4-8-4   #2610 *82*, #2602 *107*,
        #2626 *43, 109, 137*, #2608 *135*

Locomotives, diesel
F-units   #6510 *39*, #6504 *138*, #5403 *138*,
       #6706A *139*
Gas-electric   *126, 143, 145*

PACIFIC COAST RAILWAY
Locomotives, steam
0-6-0   #17 *155*
2-8-0   #16 *152-153*, #12 *155*, #15 *155, 157*,
        #16 *156*, #14 *157*
4-4-0   #18 *154*

UNION PACIFIC
Locomotives, steam
2-8-2   #2510 *101*
4-6-2   #3225 *92*, #3201 *80*
4-8-2   #7014 *101*, #7818 *122, 125*, #7017 *128*

Locomotives, diesel
M-10,000   *87*

SKAGIT RAILWAY   *158-159*

TRACTION & MISC.
Puget Sound Electric *146-148*
New waterfront trolley *151*
North Coast Lines (Everett to Seattle) *149-150*
Seattle Electric *90*
Seattle Municipal Ry. *72, 82-86, 92*
Seattle & Rainier Valley *74, 89*
#19 carline in Seattle *70-71*

CB&Q E-8 diesel *117*
SP&S F-unit *118-119*